T0161461

SISYPHUS, OUTDONE.

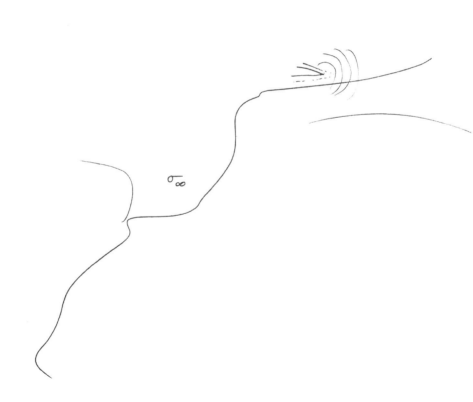

SISYPHUS, OUTDONE.

Theatres of the Catastrophal

NATHANAËL

Nightboat Books, Callicoon, New York 2012

the shot sounds beforehand ahead / of just
after, its sound like a / door with no house
standing wide open still
—Inger Christensen

On pourra peut-être démontrer le caractère
inéluctable de certaines catastrophes, comme
la maladie ou la mort. La connaissance ne
sera plus nécessairement une promesse de
réussite, ou de survie; elle pourra être tout
aussi bien la certitude de notre échec, de
notre fin.
—René Thom

$$\frac{\partial^2 L_c}{\partial \dot{\ell}^2}\, \ddot{\ell} = \frac{\partial L_c}{\partial \ell} - \frac{\partial^2 L_c}{\partial \ell \, \partial \dot{\ell}}\, \dot{\ell}$$

There is no longer light in the house. No
glass in the windows. No one stirs and no one
stands up.
—Ingeborg Bachmann

σ_∞ — remote stress (far-field)

$L = EK - \Pi$ (potential)

$L_c = R\left\{ \mathcal{G}^{dyn}\left(n_1 + \dot{\ell}^2 n_2\right) - 2\gamma \right\}$

when $\ell = \boxed{C_{LA}t}$

surface energy

$\sigma_a = \dfrac{K_I^{dyn}}{\sqrt{2\pi r}}$

$K_I^{dyn} = k(\dot{\ell}) K_I(\ell)$

$\mathcal{G}^{dyn} = g(\dot{\ell}) G(\ell)$

crack acceleration

$r = \dfrac{K_I^{dyn^2}}{2\pi \sigma_\infty^2} \Rightarrow R(\dot{\ell}, \ell)$

σ_∞

$-\dot{\ell}_{CR}$

equation of dynamic crack growth

crack length

crack speed

$\dfrac{\partial^2 L_c}{\partial \dot{\ell}^2}\ddot{\ell} = \dfrac{\partial L_c}{\partial \ell} - \dfrac{\partial^2 L_c}{\partial \ell \partial \dot{\ell}}\dot{\ell}$

$\dot{\ell} = \dfrac{d\ell}{dt}$

$L_c = \dfrac{K_I^{dyn^2}}{\boxed{\dot{\ell}}}\left\{ \mathcal{G}^{dyn}\left(n_1 + \dot{\ell}^2 n_2\right) - 2\gamma \right\}$

$= \dfrac{\Delta l}{\dot{\ell}}$ Creep. It gets us all in the end.

$2 = \dfrac{K_I^{dyn}}{\dot{\ell}}$ or $\dfrac{1}{\dot{\ell}}$ (?)

Someone carries a door through a door. | This is demonstrable.

Still.

»

After an aftershock, there is stillness. There are reverberations and then there is stillness. The stillness itself is reverberant. Reverberant with the reverberations of the shock. I am shaken and then I am still. Instilled in me is the shakenness.

»

After assumes before, because of the way the eye is trained to look backwards to the source of a pain (une douleur), as though it traversed time progressively, as though, in pain, a pain could be charted, mapped, contained, as though a pain itself could not be maimed, for having been, once before, this thing.

»

I would like to suspend the question of before, as it has no bearing on the question of the aftershock. It bears its weight of memory as lost memory and time as lost time. Lost and thus not locatable on a scale of before and after, on a seismic scale of measurable disturbances. Implicit in the aftershock is before's probability, arguable as temporal necessity. In this instance, the one which joins us here, still, there is not before; there is only the door.

»

After an aftershock, there is stillness in the fault plane. With and without (visible) fault lines. The fault may be mine. In keeping with the fault, out of line. Seismically, I presume— I know nothing of such things—the stillness to be measurable, the way tremors are. Seismically, I presume again, for it not to be possible, ever, for the earth not to move. For the rest of us not to be moved by it. Every which way: still.

»

(The temporality of my admission is suspect, admittedly.)

»

On a French tongue, the aftershock is pronounced *réplique*. I will speak now, instead,
to the *réplique* leaving the matter of before
and after aside, extricating myself from
the misplacement of time in catastrophe. A
réplique which is the earth's answer, shall we
say, to its own misdemeanour. What it offers
as reply, as *réplique*, to what is now, which
is after all an instance of after, and as such
unrecognisable.

»

Some examples of unrecognisable:

Ilse Bing's 1931 *Self-portrait with Leica* in
which what is seen is also what is seeing.
In which the seeing comes into the eye from
outside, turning the eye away from its *cible*,
from its point of seeing, in which the face, thus
apprehended, is always already still, distilled
into light particulate, chafing the cornea into
sharp relief.

Umbo's 1928 *Sinister Street* in which the
shadow flattens the plane of sight, levelling
wall and street to a single vertiginous layer
of suffering, in which creature or construction

and corresponding shadow—animal, walker, cart—are temporally, structurally, undifferentiable. Suffering because of the heat. Standing and suffering.

Also Vieira da Silva's 1949 painting, *Gare Saint-Lazare*, whose reciprocal text might be this passage from Ingeborg Bachmann's *Franza*: "Yet as far as we're concerned the train can travel on, for what is written about it will be spoken, the train will travel on, since it is asserted that it exists. For the facts that make the world real—these depend on the unreal in order to be recognized by it."

Or da Silva's 1964 *Stèle* which seems to identify the infinitessimal seisms present in the frame, perhaps even provoked by the frame's imposition of limitation, the stelæ forming a dispersing flotilla of some undecided material between liquid and slate, these archipelagic strata trying to constitute themselves amid an unintended blur of chroma with modernity's signature: speed.

»

Standing and suffering as in exists. As in the

train exists.

»

The geographer Michel Lussault hands me this: "...le verbe exister reprend sa significa-cation première, si l'on veut bien revenir à l'étymologie d'*ex-istere*. *Sistere*, qui dérive de la racine indo-européenne *sta*, qui veut dire se tenir debout, immobile (d'où vient le latin stare), signifie placer et/ou se placer. Exister c'est donc placer et/ou se placer « *ex* » —hors de: à la fois se placer et se déplacer, bref agir pour trouver ses (bonnes) places." [1]

1   *L'homme spatial*, 33.

»

"Qui veut dire se tenir debout, immobile", which means to stand still.

»

It is raining in.

»

Unrecognisable might also be Robert Häusser's *The 21 Doors of Benito Mussolini* (1983). Twenty-one doors from Il Duce's villa for the twenty-one years of Mussolini rule. The doors (continue to) exist and the memory of these accompanies the dwellings lost to—razed by —a fascist politics of *sventramenti*, or disembowelment, after Haussmann's *éventrement*. Twenty-one doors for some twenty-thousand dwellings demolished in Florence alone between 1927 and 1931. For which the evicted inhabitants sometimes stood still for one last photograph; cumulatively, these photographs "are the hasty, semi-official record of what was demolished and they were usually taken when the buildings were already gutted and the shells stood haunting and lifeless, hollow window holes like gouged eyes, a carcass picked clean of life and memory."[2]

2   Spiro Kostof, 10.

»

If the body occupies a space, is the body itself not a space? Is the body occupied by the space it occupies? Thus doubling its occupancy rate? And the rate of temporal decay? Jacques Derrida writes "car quand je dis corps,

3   *Chaque fois unique la fin du monde*, 209.

j'entends le corps vivant."[3] "When I say body, I mean the living body." Me, I am not sure I am able to make this distinction. The seism says otherwise. The seism belies durability. Even this breath, which I take while writing these lines, is pushed out by other breath. I breathe out, I expel myself. The tremor in this instance is expectant (expectorant). What space the body occupies is still and already occupied by the expectation of its riddance.

»

4   "Mais un séisme, en soi, n'est pas un phénomène social." Michel Lussault, *L'homme spatial*, 20.

Un séisme en soi. [4] A seism in (it)self. An ontology of foreclosed possibility. Of foregone eventuality. The single, perhaps even singular, certainty, is the conjuncture, in the body, living or not living, of shakenness and still-ness, of tremulous seismicity. None of this is decided.

»

Lussault insists: "Mais un séisme, en soi, n'est pas un phénomène social."

»

What I misremember is this: "L'espace n'est pas un séisme en soi." I repeat this to myself for the two seasons between reading and recording that line and this text. Two seasons of mnemonic fault, of disavowed repeatability. In my ear, l'espace n'est pas un séisme en soi. Space is not a seism in (it)self. I am prepared to conjecture otherwise. I begin to prepare my argument, but it is argument only with myself. With my misremembrance of a line attributed to the spatialist, Lussault, when really my argument is with the unreal, my fault is else-where. Now I am elsewhere with my fault, a displaced comma, a fragment of a phrase, extracted like a small piece of glass from the skin, this: un séisme en soi. A seism in (it)self.

»

What outdid Sisyphus.

»

In Martin Buber's "dream of the double-cry" what comes in from outside is the cry's double. In the dream there is a cry, from without the dream comes another cry to join it; this cry's undefinable perfection, according to Buber, is attributable to its being "already there". The conjoined cries are the seismic matter of the dream, whose tremors reverberate into a state of waking and remembering. Repeatedly, through the years. A rejoinder, per Buber's English translator, Ronald Gregor-Smith, joining again.

»

The réplique is dialogical, combative, echoic, duplicitous. In theatre, it is simply what is said. This theatre, however, is catastrophal. It is a catastrophized theatre, reiterated in and outside of the body, with and without language.

»

Duplicitous for its replications.

»

A theatre of the catastrophal is a theatre of reiterative ending. With its etymological gesturings toward the conclusive and the turn, the overturn, the downturn, the catastrophe's finality is thwarted now that we live among so many mirrors. [5]

»

5   Catastrophe [a. Gr. καταστροφή overturning, sudden turn, conclusion, f. κατα-στρέφω to overturn, etc., f. κατά down + στρέφω to turn.] 1. 'The change or revolution which produces the conclusion or final event of a dramatic piece' (J.); the dénouement. 2. 'A final event; a conclusion generally unhappy' (J.); a disastrous end, finish-up, conclusion, upshot; overthrow, ruin, calamitous fate. 3. An event producing a subversion of the order or system of things. b. esp. in Geol. A sudden and violent change in the physical order of things, such as a sudden upheaval, depression, or convulsion affecting the earth's surface, and the living beings upon it, by which some have supposed that the successive geological periods were suddenly brought to an end. 4. A sudden disaster, wide-spread, very fatal, or signal. (In the application of exaggerated language to misfortunes it is used very loosely.) *Oxford English Dictionary.*

6   *Absence Where As*, 76.

"Turns (in) me, returns (to) me, turns me out." [6]

»

Réplique: Spatially, the room is finite. What enters through the body, through the speaking voice, orients thought away from its confines toward an exacerbated awareness of endlessly forming breaches. This is no threshold: it is a reiterated collision that belies the possibility of situation.

»

It is reigning (me) in.

»

What is, or might be, seismic about speaking. Pulse at the navel. The higher it rises, the closer to the heart, the nearer to cardiac arrest. The violent stilling of the heart. "Tu entends venir la catastrophe", Derrida. Again: "le cœur te bat." [7] Where the voice becomes tangled with the heart, the beat ceases to be discernible. It accelerates to catch up with the thing that appears to escape. From the heart, through the mouth, into the world. Hold it back.

»

The mouth of the world.

»

The twain world is comprised of shreds of each and each, of disembodied interlopers, myopic spectators with our noses pressed against the glass of our desires, of our trembling intimacies.

»

When you walk through the door, you walk into me.

»

"Une phrase c'est un muscle." So says French playwright Noëlle Renaude. She says this on the radio as I am listening.

»

This musculature is historical. A sentence

is what muscles its way into my mouth and forces itself out. How will the time of death be determined. Who will measure its implacability. There is no instrument for this, not even the seismograph can tell. The double of death is death again.

»

The double of death is death (in) itself. The corruptions of existence register in the vital body as evidence of temporal decay. The machines attached to the body ignore, for example, the displacement of weight in a horse's corpse as it runs its last run, as it outlasts itself, as it is undone. To this the only possible rejoinder is the réplique. I ask myself. [8]

»

8   "If by chance we speak to mirrors, it is perhaps less for narcissistic reasons than out of a desire for dead time separating us from the battering voices we carry." *Absence Where As*, 48.

There is no cell that is not undivided.

»

Réplique: The thought of thinking is an occurrence of not undivided. In a seismic body the sexes are neither conjoined nor distinct. They tremble at the thought of thinking themselves into a shape. A shape that might eventually be recognisable. Which means to stand still. The sex of the sexes is inchoate. Once it is born it is alone with its birth, it is without genitors, it has only its death to look forward to. This is as it writes itself into existence.

»

The reproducibility of the genitors is a non-sequitur.

»

Inchoate is hermaphroditic. What is unspoken (for).

»

Hermaphroditic is unrecognisable. Claude Cahun's *Que me veux-tu?* (1928) for example. What do you want from me. The question asks itself. It takes pains taking pleasure from itself. It marks the world made and unmakes it.

»

This is what happens: "They kill the original, by discovering that the original was already dead." [9]

»

I go in search of the other shoe.

»

What gives way is given away. In translation the pieces are not counted, nor are they accounted for. The translation itself is unfounded. On the rise of what ruin does it take its place. The promontory as overturn and undertow. The littoral whose demarcations are suffused with the refuse of cities, their refusals, marking edge of water and land as trash. This is as I understand translatability. In its manifold dismantlings, disintegrations. This is the part that is not spoken or fretted over. What cannot be imparted. The fraction of infraction. The

9   Paul de Man on Walter
     Benjamin's "The Task of
     the Translator".

point at which there is nothing left, nothing to motion over, nothing to speak for.

»

A translation, which might be unforgivable were it not for this: what is to forgive when nothing is given.

»

Someone carries a door through a door. This is demonstrable.

»

There are two doors. A door in a doorway. On this threshold, there is an absence of limits, an exacerbated falsehood of traversal. What possibility exists in the space occupied by two doors enters into the body as foreclosure and eventuality. The madness is what pulls at liver and groin simultaneously. I might touch this surface until it is soaked through, suppurating. The pores opened by fractal explosions, each of which registers as a quiet stutter that enters the atmosphere.

»

10   Paul Virilio, *Bunker Archeology*, 15.

"Trap doors open in the cement floor," [10]

»

A door which opens onto no room. A room whose door is only an approximation of a door. The ante-chamber, for example, of the "torturable body" Brecht attributed to Walter Benjamin. "When you destroyed a torturable body." [11] The accusative "you" whose function may unwittingly collapse accusation and interpellation into the space of a word. As though by "you", grief's fault might be attributed, assigned, a way of measuring loss with address: you. Egregious, éloge.

11   "On the Suicide of the Refugee, W.B.," tr. John Willett. The French translation attaches the accusation more directly to the body in its designation, yours: "ton corps torturable." Cited by Ilsa Trudel in *L'ange assassiné*, 38; tr. undisclosed.

»

12   Paul Virilio, *Bunker Archéologie*, 22.

"Des trappes s'ouvrent dans le sol de ciment," [12]

»

In a book, as it is being written, a room is traversed. From end to end toward the door. There is a person who moves from window to door. Who is running the self out. Reiteratively. There is a room and there is a war. [13]

13   *We Press Ourselves Plainly.*

»

These perambulations are catastrophal in that they register the ends over and over again.

»

This is what Sisyphus saw. He stood still at memory's gates. [14]

14   "...memory opens all its gates and yet is not open wide enough," Friedrich Nietzsche, *Untimely Considerations*, 78.

»

Did he pry them open.

»

The permanence of catastrophes: philosopher-mathematician René Thom is before both doors, observing "les modes par lesquels on

15   René Thom. *Prédire n'est pas expliquer*, 22.

peut envoyer un espace dans un autre." [15] The door in itself is a discontinuous phenomenon, in that it opens simultaneously onto nothing and onto itself.

»

"When a person very close to us is dying, there is (we dimly apprehend) something in the months to come that—much as we should have liked to share it with him—could happen only through his absence. We greet him, at the last, in a language that he already no longer understands." [16]

16   Walter Benjamin. "One-Way Street," tr. Edmund Jephcott, in *Selected Writings, Volume 1*, 450.

»

For Noëlle Renaude, the disaster is prolific, dynamic: "on décide de son désastre quand on est sur le plateau." It is willed and it is willful. In a theatre of the catastrophal one's disaster is decided with temperamental exigency against the inclemency of the réplique, subsumed into the woodwork. This stage (plateau). This delinquency.

»

What does it do to one's ipseity to say, in the first person, *I am dying?* Is this the equivalent of cancelling oneself out? For a tailor, it might be a needle ground in several indiscernible pieces into the bones of her wrist. None of this is written, nor is it written out. The predications may be predictable, but only as after thought.

»

A theatre of reiterative ending is also a theatre of translatability. In translation the broken mirror stands in for every possible mirror, though it is none of these. It is not Cocteau's watery passageway into an oneiric world, nor Marie-Françoise Plissart's mise en abyme of photography's seductions, but a mirror that is shattered over and over until the mouth, filled with glass, is only capable of speaking interruption. This mouth is not concerned with rupture per se nor with dissolution but with the mounting urgency (insurgency) of its shattering recursion. It speaks, not to be spoken or heard, but out of a necessity that is separate from language. The necessity of a mouth without a world.

»

Still the mouth is catastrophal. It kisses catastrophe into the world.

»

…

II

17 Ingeborg Bachmann. *The Book of Franza*. 3.

"Ways of dying also include crimes." [17]

»

I feel myself of another time, as though there were other time.

»

18 "Over", i.e. over and again.

Side by side or superimposed, Paul Virilio's *Tilting* bunker and Michal Rovner's *Outside #2* exacerbate—they reiterate—the time of decay: Rovner's over-exposures [18] bring to the surface of the Bedouin house its temporal degradation, granting it oblique equivalency with the bunker sinking into the sand. Rovner slows time, measuring its imprint, extruding from the house in the desert the implanted time of accelerated degradation. What Virilio's bunker exposes (documents) Rovner's antici-pates by ennervation. There is the subjective disclosure of the subject's disintegration in time, in a frame. What I see, in each instance, is not a house nor a bunker, but the work of time, the anticipation and accomplishment of death's (de)composition.

36

19   Hervé Guibert. *Le mausolée des amants*, 187.

Un événement de lumière. [19]

»

An event of light which is or might be a storm. Light storming the house in the desert. Light, which in this instance, is, has the potential to be, catastrophal. Bringing about. Standing the house more still.

»

The photograph lacks definition. A world (worlds) undefined.

»

The photograph does not lack defintion. It draws out that which by definition is undefined. Undiscerned by instrument. Absent of designation.

»

Do I kiss it back.

»

Death's (de)composition is (also) a theatre of war.

»

What are we waiting for.

»

In Guy Hocquenghem's aspiration to object-less desire [20] and Hervé Guibert's consideration of subjectless photography [21] there is the intimation of the removal of a self in order to unburden a context of its context. A voice without language or touch without touch.

»

20   Guy Hocquenghem. *Le désir homosexuel*, 121. « [Le désir homosexuel] est la pente vers la trans-sexualité par la disparition des objets et des sujets, le glissement vers la découverte qu'en sexe, tout communique. »

21   Guibert. « Comme la photographie peut n'être qu'un événement de lumière, sans sujet (et c'est le moment où elle est le plus photographie), j'aimerais un jour me lancer dans un récit qui ne serait qu'un événement d'écriture, sans histoire, et sans ennui, une véritable aventure. »

22   Jean-François Lyotard, *La Chambre sourde*, 41.

"La sexualité indépendante de tout objet... sujet et rejet même." [22]

»

In the last of language, language is subjectless. It ruins itself against an embarrassing
hope for more. Its perversion is less than this.
Less than its desire for itself.

»

Its rejection.

»

A ruined language is a language with neither
subject nor object. It says nothing (or too
much) of where it has been. Intimacy is, in this
instance, intimation: "La ruine nous conduit à
une expérience qui est celle du sujet dessaisi,
et paradoxalement il n'y a pas d'objet à cette
expérience." [23]

23   Sophie Lacroix. *Ruine*, 52.

»

Who was there in the first place.

»

The door is always open. [24] This might be

24   In Hell, Sartre leaves the
door open.

History's *proviso*. An inhospitable hospitality. Suspect and ill at ease. [25]

25 "Such that the question for me becomes a very simple architectural one, it is the question of the doorway, in French, l'embrasure, with its attendant gesturings toward desire. Who is standing at this door? Who opens or closes it. And what might this threshold become if we were to cross it, to cross it out?" "Some notes on death and the burning of buildings".

»

The I might be a catastrophist. Taking turns. Turning out.

»

Seismically speaking, a split self is rendered unavowably speechless. Self without self. Irreferent.

»

Is it for lack of place.

»

Or: a siteless retort, pronounced out of place.

The site ridded of seeing may be a way away from pronouncement. Built or borne.

»

This is Heidegger's declaration: "The proper sense of *bauen*, namely dwelling, falls into oblivion." [26] This is the case, also, of the proper senses. Undwelled, obliviated.

26 "Building Dwelling Thinking," in *Basic Writings*, 326.

»

The impropriety with which, for example, we are secluded.

For example: we bereave the sense of our freedoms.

»

A house which is built into its destruction.

»

RY King's photographic dissolve marks the paper immutable. Immutable in that it is always imbricated in a mechanism of deterioration. In this improper sense, the image is not separable from its degradation. Its substances are both paper and light. Thus they are neither, as they run into each other.

»

The bird, in this instance, which is scarcely discernible, is in a field of apparent surfaces. It comprises the surface by which it becomes visible, an irregularity on a structure of hay bales in a field of depleted colour. The photograph misdirects its intention. It intends for me to fall in.

In to America.

»

The identification of a site is improper in that it precludes situation. It steadies itself in a blur which I take to be my eyes. In this sense I become the photograph proper. It is in the skin and in the paper and against a wall. The door, here, is diminished, but not foregone.

»

The fall is ever a truncation of fallout. In this theatre of scarce forms, the photograph intimates residual catastrophe.

»

It is nowhere to be seen. It is this which the photograph comes between.

»

As gas mask or oxygen. Those particular theatres.

44

»

27   Stephen Motika.
      Arrival and At Mono.

"What is architecture's error?" [27]

»

That particulate which may be granular. What fastens the paper to its skin. A regional deference.

»

It comes with a number, assigned to a cal-cined human body which is incommunicable: When it says "...j'ai besoin de catastrophes, de coups de théâtre" [28] it abandons sense.

28   Guibert, 262.

»

The lake is up to my knees in November.

»

In calx.

»

The time of the photograph is (always) after. This imprecision accommodates the numerous successions, the end upon seismic end. In a time without time, un(re)countable: still. In this, it is a perfect crime, "l'anéantissement anéanti, la fin ... privée d'elle-même."[29]

29   Lyotard, 29.

»

The photographic occasion, its occasional reoccurrence makes incontrovertible "l'épouvante lucide de la redite." [30]

30   Lyotard, 39.

»

When you touch it, is it said?

»

"Le désastre est séparé, ce qu'il y a de plus séparé." [31]

31   Maurice Blanchot, *L'Écriture du désastre*, 7.

»

Réplique: The chairs change place. The armchair is taken out. The other one, however, the green one, is transported here as well as the rope that fastens the arm that's coming away. In addition, there are two white painted chairs on a back, wooden chairs, despite a dislike for painted wood, one day and then the next, they stay there, at the entranceway, latent chairs, which haven't assumed their function as chairs, but hold their place. The chairs are all empty and yet upon arrival it is impossible to sit down, the two cats occupy the twelve chairs including the bed.

»

Se-parare, without making ready.

»

Is it found or is it given or is it taken from what was (already) taken away? [32]

»

32 A small stack of letters adddressed variously yields the following occurrences: (1) But it made me feel once again like The Murderer; (2) ...and so here is another opportunity for me to feel like I've committed a murder; (3) Je n'en peux plus d'être le meurtrier; (4) So much that it seems I've committed a

murder by coming here;
(5) ...and so I think that I
must be a murderer of sorts,
a murderer of people and
of cities; (6) Because I have
come to think of death as
murder, and our complicity;
(7) Etc.

For example, Sir Thomas Bouch, who had not yet been knighted in 1870, designed the wrought and cast iron two and a quarter mile Tay Railway Bridge without calculation of the winter gales over the firth into his design; the bridge collapsed scarcely a year and a half after its construction. It collapsed under a train full of people. The structurally deficient Bridge 9340 over the Mississippi River in Minneapolis collapsed in August 2007, at the height of traffic, forty years after its inauguration. The indiscretion is in history and in materiality, each of which may be cited as deficient in structure and design.

»

Is a catastrophic failure a failure of time, a tempest unaccounted for in number or incident. [33]

33   "Une syncope dans le sang."
Carnet de désaccords, 97.

»

For body, substitute bodies. Reiterate indiscretions.

»

"Ce que l'on appelle usuellement une forme, c'est toujours, en dernière analyse, une discontinuité qualitative sur un certain fond continu." [34] Thom's definitions misdirect substitution. He clarifies: the foundation of a problem in any of the sciences is an aporia. For once, the disappearances can be accounted for. Whether or not they manifest as (retinal) discontinuities or continuous underpinnings.

»

Mathematically speaking: something moves over something that doesn't move. Conversely, something that doesn't move touches something that does. There is no equivalency between the horse's last run and the photographic fix. One moves without the other. Something is torn.

»

34   Thom, 35.

"Because the geometry / we seek is beyond coordination," [35]

35   Michael O'Leary, *Along the Chess Pavilion*.

»

There is no perfect isolate. Simply a proclivity for destructions of all kinds. The aleatory conjunction of Fourier's Arcades with Benjamin's (sometimes contested) suicide is arguable against an ethics of encounter's hermaphrodisms. [36] But there is no possible proof of this. If Benjamin considered suicide at the age of forty, is the fortieth age the end (of) time?

36   Encounter, from the O.F. *encontre*, masculine or feminine: of undecided form.

»

Neuter, it is said. But neuter is without desire.

The city presented a sky that demanded an ocean, but there were none of these.

»

To say "all kinds" is to invite various imprecisions. Benjamin's lost attaché case is perhaps the most convincing piece of evidence.

»

37 The Old Tay Bridge
    in Eiffel's eye.

A mode of somatic interrogation. [37]

»

For Derrida, it might be Nietzsche's lost umbrella.

»

38 Paul Celan,
    tr. Michael Hamburger.

"It is, / I know, not true / that we lived, there moved, / blindly, no more than a breath between / there and not-there," [38]

»

Because of its lostness.

»

The Roman amphitheatre is a spectacular place of slaughter. "La distance est immense entre la conviction personnelle et la démonstration:" [39] A theatre, which continues in the present to command murder, is complicit with the injunction to (an) end. We are *in the act*.

»

Taken aback. [40]

»

39 Thom, 72.

40 Following a public execution, which he had attended with some conviction, Albert Camus's father goes home, doesn't speak, lies down on the bed, and begins immediately to vomit. "Ma mère raconte seulement qu'il rentra en coup de vent, le visage bouleversé, refusa de parler, s'étendit un moment sur le lit et se mit tout d'un coup à vomir. (...) Au lieu de penser aux enfants massacrés, il ne pouvait plus penser qu'à ce corps pantelant qu'on venait de jeter sur une planche pour lui couper le cou." *Réflexions sur la peine capitale*, 143–144.

This is not calculated into the displacement of materials and surfaces, but in their resistance, perhaps, to being moved. Removed. The thwarted Archimedean resolve (to drown).

»

In the Sisyphus text, there is talk of murder.

»

41   James Joyce, *Ulysses*, 25.

"Yes, a disappointed bridge." [41]

»

It isn't for want or lack. In the visage, the eyes are become too wide, too languid and imbecilic. Is this what it is (also) to look. "You behold in me, [...], a horrible example of free thought." [42]

42   Joyce, 21.

»

It seems vital now, that we do this.

»

43 André Malraux, *Lazare*, 422. "L'histoire efface jusqu'à l'oubli des hommes."

If not for any reason, other than the one cited. If it is true, for example, that "Il ne reste rien de l'évènement," [43] then photography, in Guibert's projection, is predicated, first, on forgetting, and perhaps synchronously on nothing. In which instance, nothing, is what comes of light, as it happens. [44]

44 A paper which evidences its burning.

»

Green: "...into the subject of poisonous colours. It has been found that arsenic is sometimes used in the preparation of some wall papers, especially though not exclusively, the green ones. This has been known to produce effects of poisoning on the occupiers. It is almost the only case in which the air of our rooms is liable to actual poisoning for the effects of air that is foul from any other cause are not..." [45]

45 Cecil Scott Burgess, *Architecture, Town Planning and Community*, 76.

»

Historically speaking, our nothing is in our forgottenness. [46]

46 "first a razor then a fact." Michael Palmer, *Sun*, 6.

»

For Malraux, it is in the death count: "Le jour anniversaire de ma quarantième année, lorsque je passais clandestinement la ligne de démarcation avec le chat noir, j'aurais voulu être né la veille." [47]

47   *Lazare*, 479.

»

His year of quarantine.

»

The geometry of the poison is qualitative. [48]

48   "On n'échappe pas au continu." Thom, 66.

»

In a logic, then, of photographic eventuality, we forget nothing.

»

"Un jour, toutes les photos seront dissoutes, le papier photo n'impressionnera plus, ne réagira plus, sera chose morte." [49]

49   Guibert, 168.

»

"It is my want that it is looked at closely and in light, please." [50]

50 RY King.

III

If there were a concordance between the place of birth and the place of death,

»

The photograph makes more of disavowal. For example: "I admit to closing more books than I open." [51] It disavows the line and it draws a line. A face, for example. It is not that I cry, but the summary made, by the photograph, of proximities. The face, for example, driven into its pain. And the impression (sense) of leaving with one's eyes. As though looking were a form of desistance. Mine, first, because I am the one looking.

»

Between the mailbox and the train is the attendant question: is it possible to photograph the sound of the train. To move the sound into a frame.

»

Posed differently, I might scratch with Christine

51   *Absence Where As*, 13.

Lavant at the little door, "tandis que je gratte à la petite porte, /

»

52   *Un art comme le mien*
       n'est que vie mutilée, 208.

mendiant dans la ferme des souffrances." [52]
The transposition to a different key.

»

53   *I have just this instant come*
       upon the most wonderful
       concordance; the unwitting
       compression of the English
       phrase "in time", yields the
       French: intime, which means
       intimate—adjectivally and
       substantively. That intimacy
       could be—is—substantive—//
       self-existent—// there is tea
       now in the unbroken pot; (From
       a letter, sent. Henceforth,
       unattributed quotations are
       indicative of such letters.)

In time. [53]

»

Thus creating the following tautology: I might scratch with Christine Lavant at the little door, while I scratch at the little door. The erstwhile hinge is tandis que; it groans as does wood that is swollen.

»

Ferme, which is close, close. The close of
sufferings. Misindicating the substantive in
favour of other, mitigating, proximities. That
ferme might also signal a trap door in a
cement floor, at a particularly vexing moment
of redirected intention.

»

A translation is not a tautology. It is something else.

»

Doubled (over).

»

Nor is it citation.

»

The fantasy of (this) translation is that it is
repeatable.

»

For example: "Your voice lingers here in the fore-cast."

»

No assurance is given as to the qualification of the sound as it is scratched onto the retina.

»

54   "não compreendo o olho, e tento chegar perto." Hilda Hilst, *A obscena Senhora D*, 21.

The eye itself is not sound. [54]

»

A complete set of small green encyclopædia. Each of the XXV volumes is green and each spine has gilt lettering and is imprinted with the outline of the Empire State Building. All XXV Empire State buildings fit into a small box, which is carried comfortably under the arm for several blocks. Published in 1931 [55], they occupy approximately two linear feet of floor space, and are each four inches tall.

55   The same year that Geli Raubal, Hitler's niece, committed suicide.

»

Tautology: the Empire State Building is inaugurated in 1931. The encyclopædia account for this. Which is to say that I invent it.

»

I invent the concordance in and of the present.

»

"And here the time of memory is precisely the time I am describing." [56]

»

Gunpowder green tea in this America.

»

It is the concordance which invents [57] the present.

»

The sound and the rail line. The low wall

56   Wittgenstein, 18.

57   —contrives.

and the fence, clipped in places, allowing for unauthorized foot traffic. Covered over and clipped again, such that the fence bears visible stitchings replenishing holes which are less visible and apt to disappear. The distances are altered precisely by these alterations. It is then possible to posit the disappearances of the walkers who walk in anticipation of these breaches. The removal of foothold and course.

»

Over three kilometres of undocumented passage multiplied by the number of traversals.

»

Thus: "I know what I am looking for without [...] having to exist."
.

»

Wittgenstein's injunction—the *having to*—corroborates his certainty. What is obliterated with the knowledge of what is sought is the self-seeking. To my unsound eye, the repeated phrase, "what I am looking for" is excised from the page as I tender it to myself, removing ontology from view leaving certainty (alone). The reinstated text translated by Raymond Hargreaves and Roger White renders: "I know what I am looking for without what I am looking for having to exist." In the time lapse, delay, the corrected version reads wrong, and it is the negative which remains: "without what I am looking for."

»

The concordance is in: without.

»

Then what is the relationship between obsolescence and the negative?

»

"When other socialist countries discarded Marxism-Leninism as a way of life, the GDR ceased to exist altogether." [58]

»

58 Karl Gernot Kuehn, *Caught*, ix.

In a falsely posed problem of improbability, two people carry one body through two doors. Understood thus, one body is transported with difficulty by two people. The body is the body of a person, carried first through one door, then another. They disappear with the body, past the turnstile. After, they are there again; it is the same body. The person is not dead to begin with. First, there is a person, then there is a person, dead; the bearers of the dead do not know it. Neither at the beginning nor at the end. They are carrying a person. I watch as they do this. They enter, go out, the body is so big, bigger than itself, so heavy, heavier than itself, a leg drags, the bearers falter. Back and then forth. They go through the swinging door, the pair of glasses on the face, knocked askew.

»

A door open in two directions at once.

»

I made wishes for each of the horses, and drank green tea, and wrote you ardently.

»

The body functions as its own anachronism. To posit a temporality is a way of overlooking time.

»

59 "; un sentiment sans objet, comme l'angoisse, et qui invente son objet." Malraux, 504.

For example, I am writing Sisyphus. [59]

»

Is a field taken taken different than a face?

»

60 According to OED, an obsolete acception of site is "Care or sorrow; grief, trouble of any kind." A rare usage, *to make site* signifies to lament, mourn.

61 Suzanne Jacob, 82.

62 "L'espace y est la pensée même". Jean Baudrillard, *Amérique*, 22.

Made or unmade the site [60] proves unthinkable. "—Je voudrais pouvoir chialer par les neuf fenêtres et les trois portes de cette maison sans héritier." [61] It is precisely where space begins to think that it makes itself unthinkable. [62]

»

What prohibition prevents such bawling by architecture's apertures.

»

That one should abide such dwelling.

»

For the lingerer who stays in (a) place courts a variety of obsolescences. [63] "The deep parts producing the shadows, and the high parts producing white." [64]

»

Réplique: There are such distances, between windows and doors, as have not (yet) been accounted for.

»

Without having to exist.

»

63   Namely the obsolescence of this acception of *to linger*: to dwell, abide, stay (in a place). OED.

64   From the "Photogravure" entry in the *Funk & Wagnalls New Standard Encyclopedia*, 1931.

This America, for example, which, demonstrably, is not a signifier. It is the negative (in) itself.

»

The negative of itself.

»

65 Bazin: "...sauver l'être par l'apparence."

Were it (not) for the appearances of being. [65] An ontological distressor.

»

The charge of the thing set between thing and thing speaks amply of the human's manifest need for substraction from situation, for the disavowal of (reflexive) emotion.

»

Whether the post scriptum is (also) a post mortem. [66]

66 "When I die, it's hardly likely that someone will write a quartet dedicated to my memory. So I decided to write

»

it myself. One could write on
the frontispiece, 'Dedicated
to the author of this quartet.'"
Dmitri Shostakovich, in a
letter to Isaak Glikman,
July 16, 1960.

In 1944 there is already Shostakovich. The notes accompanying the Sonata for viola and piano, Opus 147 in C Minor make mention of "a more private grief. " In "the extreme pain in Shostakovich's composing hand", it is not the poliomyelitis that I intimate, but another, far less literal pain.

»

What is a literal pain.

»

A glass feather and a stone bird. The shadow lifts the light into the blighted crevasse. In this, the photograph is timed—*anachronic*. "[Elle] pourrait être pensé[e] comme un moment, comme un battement rythmique de la méthode, fût-il son moment de syncope." [67] Its beaten wing shattered in the eye that finds itself looking. The catastrophal measure of distances is a surrogate for the ill expressed

67   Georges Didi-Huberman,
     Devant le temps, 21–22.

71

68 "when by its remoteness, we fail to discern it as a whole." *The Notebooks of Leonardo Da Vinci*, 127.

69 *Ibid.*, 129.

inadequacy before temporal havoc. [68] "As the chamber of the eye is very dark," [69] a shadow, thus cast, corresponds to a body cast out, its casting a stratagem for holding time (still). In this, the syncope is gleaned from the eye's tattered movement.

»

"Thus does the photograph's more habitual temporal acception (rigor mortis) give over to something, I want to say: more musical."

»

A stifled lurch into movement.

»

For example: Rachel Whiteread's Judenplatz *mahnmal* mausoleum pulses with untold bodies. The implacable stone cast verges on monumental collapse; in the square it is contained by the square, which, in this instance is not mathematical. Unless it is a calculated atrocity. To bear the angular weight of this architecture is to argue an objectionable measure of dust.

»

A seismic illusion. Not, in this instance, the illusion of a seism, but the allusion to the seism (in) itself. A disproportionate density.

»

The body is so big, bigger than itself, so heavy, heavier than itself.

»

"Mais, une pensée n'est pas tout à fait une personne," [70]

70   Blanchot, *L'arrêt de mort*, 55.

»

In keeping with its vastness, we are its evacuees.

IV

Let this take the form of a castigation, then.

»

73 (which invents—*contrives*—its own object)

74 "Pendant la Résistance, j'ai possédé du cyanure pendant deux ans. Lorsque Londres nous l'a distribué, je me suis demandé si la scène de mon livre deviendrait prémonitoire." Malraux, 516.

A given end [73]: London's distribution, for example, to members of the Résistance, of cyanide. [74]

»

75 What Baudrillard terms *la sortie de l'histoire* arrives, in English, through Geoff Dyer, as *the end of history*. What emergency is belied in this translation? Amérique's coming out of history is not exchangeable against a Marxian end-time, in the imperfect exchange value of languages. *La sortie de l'histoire* pressed into the well-worn habit of recitable theory loses awkwardness in favour of misdirection. We are on our way out. Which is to say reiteratively *aggrieved*, not, alas, finished.

76 Maynard, 193.

Might one speak, in such instances, of outcomes, [75]

»

"or horses with all four feet off the ground." [76]

»

"La distinction entre risques 'naturels' et risques anthropiques, par exemple, devient difficile à établir du fait de la transformation croissante des milieux bio-physiques, sauf dans quelques situations simples comme les séismes ou les éruptions volcaniques." The seism is conspicuously absent from Jacques Lévy and Michel Lussault's *Dictionnaire de la géographie et de l'espace des sociétés*. It appears only briefly in the index and under the "Risque" entry on page 804, as exemplary of "Risk (Hazard), Risiko".

»

Réplique: In using the singular to designate a plural, is the number misadequated.

»

The repetitions of loss, for example.

»

Repetition.

»

The practice of which precludes perfectibility. In other words, it cannot be counted.

»

In a register of operative freedoms, a death count is seized at four times one thousand. The dissemination of this figure effectively disqualifies the particularization of the dead in unspecified areas. Expressed mathematically, what is the volume of a football field in Fallujah, notwithstanding the contraction of bodies, sheared limbs,

»

excretions.

»

Nor can it be dispensed with.

»

The geometrical shadow evinces inflection.

77 "Inflection", in OED: †2. *Optics*. The bending of a ray of light, at the edge of a body, into the geometrical shadow. Now called DIFFRACTION n. *Obs*.

[77] For the time between ten hundred street numbers, three storeys and a single longitudinal zone. A distance, say, equivalent to an equivocation. The fault is not able to be figured in the retaining wall. Practised in French, such a wall is a *mur de refend*. Taken to its letter, *re-fend*, bears the fault of its repetitions. Rending (*fendre*) again (*re-*). In an un(sp)lit theatre,

»

78 We walk, but these are scarcely surfaces.

"On marche, mais à peine sur des surfaces." [78]

»

79 *Wire_Sky_Rust.* Photograph by RY King.

The retinal detachment insists on a schism between firmaments. An instant cast backwards toward a wire sky [79], with the infernal grate fantasizing a less faint barrier against seismicity. What the eye is given to see is subdued by a mass of mismanagement, tangled detritus, an aspect of tumult, crested wave, rust and foam. The out-coming is a submersive agony.

»

She broke it. She wanted it broken and so she broke it.

»

"In our Orphic fantasies, we are each looking back. In my fantasy, we do this together, not apart."

»

Is this what history looks like.

»

Ontologically speaking, the self is in seism; it produces an instance of instantiation, a *moment of syncope*. If I stand in the way of it, I make myself substitutive, reiteratively displaceable. A translation of remove.

»

, but that I cannot take into my mouth, and it simply lies me down,

»

Not in any language.

»

80   Barbey D'Aurevilly:
     *Le dandy est d'un sexe
     intellectuel indécis.*

Syncope: In the W-C, the intellect of the sex is undecided. [80] It stands near the urinal and runs along the floor. Whatever misuses are made of the architecture are redressed by the conversion at the sink. There is no mirror, and the mind, like the mollusk, is turned inside out and tossed into the rowboat. Whatever irrelevances are noted, the body is geographically unsituated. Its squalid maltreatments are remarked upon as niceties. Simply, risen too quickly from the toilet seat, the ceiling has not time enough to readjust itself.

»

81   After Kierkegaard,
     Derrida writes: Ce
     tremblement saisit
     l'homme quand celui-ci
     devient une personne.
     Donner la mort, 21.

If a person indeed. [81]

»

Given to speaking, the terms are untenable.

Which is to say they hold the exact distances at which they are kept.

»

The distance, say, between a concrete swamp in the Middle West and a hay field in the state of Texas.

»

"I think the wound is much larger". [82]

»

82   "As an art, photography insistently gives us the pain and the boredom of seeing, and the visual desperation that can follow: *camera dolorosa*. I am interested in another sense of photography that stresses its inhumanity, its boredom, its apparently endless capacity to show us things we do not want to see." James Elkins, "Camera Dolorosa", 22.

Versions: Three English translations of *Fear and Trembling* serve to exacerbate the problem of the text's unintelligbility. The suggestion is that their aggregation may elucidate something of the original by way of simultaneity. An over-reading, say, in which palimpsestically the Danish may be divined through the layers of English prose. Instead the lure of rapprochement turns swiftly to reproach, spurning legibility. This phenomenon is perhaps best illustrated in the slide from *outpouring* to expectoration among the preliminaries.

»

83   "; for silence is both of these."
      Kierkegaard, tr. AH, 114.

A photograph makes its mute appeal [83], the unshadowed elements receding against an otherwise inexpressed desire. Its mortified composure subdued by extant animosity. The part that does speak and the part that feigns speaking.

»

84   Adolf Eichmann.

"Das war meine Aufgabe." [84]

»

It might be objected that the shadow is incremental, its advance against the raised moments of an image functioning as syncopes in the visual field.

»

Réplique: Schönberg had intended atonality as a pan-tonal system. The discrepency itself is catastrophal in that the substitutive term seems to want to *atone* for the composer's serial indistinction. Not a-, which is against, but *pan-*, a system of undifferential embracement in which the catastrophe is written into the compostion.

»

The mathematical equivalent might be presented as a discrepency between infinities. To attempt to represent the orders is to allow foremost for a récidive. [85]

85   Recurrence, or repeat offence.

»

For example: "Not all those killed have been named." [86]

86   Jan. 8, 2011, regarding the Safeway shooting in Arizona; *BBC*.

»

In a theatre of conjecture, the conjugation of catastrophes yields something of a translative procedure: it makes mortific precedent.

Symptomatically, what is said, is vitally bereft.

»

"Mais qu'est-ce à dire qu'une souffrance sans sujet?" [87]

87   Duras, *Lol V. Stein*, 23.

»

Subjectless is not without subjection.

»

Still, the distance from the garret to the sea wall is negligible. If indeed there is a lighthouse at the end of the pier, it is only reachable by sea.

»

Suffering without a subject may well be a pain in the place of a subject. If the concordance is still in without, then the concordance itself is obliterative in that it takes the form of a question of means: *mais qu'est-ce à dire—*

»

Literally: *what is (it) to say*. Speaking, in this instance, astonishes its incapabilities, rendering the subject unspeakable, expounding its unsufferability by omitting it from a language that bespeaks its omission.

»

I'll have none of it.

»

The temporal reprove is of the present, as though the having were evidence of (its) repeatability.

»

So should it be accompanied by an apology, but it does not apologise. Simply it stands in the way of that by which it is denied.

»

For example, the mollusk is pulled from the Mediterranean, turned inside out and tossed into the hull of a rowboat.

»

Given the present, how does one address an epitaph. In keeping with notions of temporal adversity, is it out of time. A practice—*répétition*—that eschews perfection, falling onto the spike, say, of its script. The architecture of which is an amalgam of false signage, interruption and invective. Already, it is a form of diminishment. It is not that inside and out are interchangeable, rather that the body is rendered adverse in its positionings.

»

History, inasmuch as it can be said to intervene, is the mute portend of a low, unfathomable pall.

»

The space itself, in which it takes place, is

88   Alexander Kluge,
     Case Histories, 44.

unsettled, "an example of which there [i]s nothing left to destroy." [88]

»

I mean that it cannot be accounted for. The remonstrations are most ardent then.

»

In 1946, the asylum functions as an panoptic observatory, in which food is spilt, a death bed is coveted, and the body inserted into the straightjacket is groped. The woman, as seen by Christine Lavant, dies unnoticed on the gurney in the room adjacent to the bathroom.

»

If the present is a measure of culpability, it is because of its immediate anteriority.

»

For example ", there is dance enormously, even when they are standing still." [89]

89   Pina Bausch.

»

It was years before I understood that he had killed it.

»

The practised "repetition at the heart of catastrophe" [90] is the rehearsal of an unmarked question in a theatre that grants no temporal reprieve. An untimely tempest, unleashed on the parts that are whited out by memory.

90 Cathy Caruth,
Unclaimed Experience, 2.

»

When Joseph Koudelka divulges: "I let others tell me what I mean" it is not that he has misspoken, but that he has spoken too soon. The 35 millimetre test prints must verify this. [91] And Michigan Avenue and the hawthorn garden.

91 "This searching for a site is unconscionable and so I have abandoned it, or it me, and I try to be attentive to these things. I keep thinking that I don't want to be the little monkey dancing for the execution squad. Like Koudelka at the Art Institute just over a week ago, or else myself—

»

89

ourselves—in the various
displays that are made of us."

Such an unburdening of epistemological responsibility is also the cynical (disconsolate) recognition of (one's) meaninglessness. It does not say so much as ask. And asking, this once, is abdicative, of catastrophe and the uncast theatre by which it is furthered.

»

92 *OED:* "(As explained by Quintilian, *apostrophe* was directed to a person *present*; modern use has extended it to the *absent* or *dead* (who are for the nonce supposed to be present);"

The still (apostrophal) [92] subject.

»

Of necessity.

»

More time for what.

aparté

If the horse lies down to sleep will it choke
in the fog?

VI (a)

, of the present that it is broken.

»

The seismic equivalent of speaking in a room might be a drowned city. Were history to ask the question of history, it might inflect the spacio-temporal condition of its asking so dramatically as to produce a question comprised only of *répliques*, or after-effects of *tout le tremblement*.

»

The suspension of the present argues for a reconsideration of the real.

»

Ionesco, by his own estimation, wrote only tragic plays. His distrust of the comic character is in its unreality: "Le personnage tragique ne change pas, il se brise; il est lui, il est réel." [93] The real, the prorogative of the present, is discredited by its impassibility. Its condition is its brokenness.

93   *Notes et contre-notes*, 249.

»

For example, México, D.F., a valley of fault lines raised some 2,240 metres above sea level, exists at the conjuncture of three techtonic plates. It evidences a discontinuous encounter (with itself).

»

Translated, the city may read thus: For Guibert, his interest in photography is predicated upon a resistance to photography. The hand at the end of the arm in *L'ami*, taken in 1980, figures this resistance.

»

Were it (simply) a matter of being said.

»

Réplique: "I laid my raincoat on the table in such a way as to be able to remove the ice axe which was in the pocket. I decided not to miss the wonderful opportunity that presented itself. The moment Trotsky began reading the article, he gave me my chance; I took out the ice axe from the raincoat, gripped it in my hand and, with my eyes closed, dealt him a terrible blow on the head." [94]

»

94   Dmitri Volkogonov, *Trotsky*, 466. When Robert Capa photographs "Leon Trotsky lecturing Danish students on the history of the Russian revolution, Copenhagen" (November 27, 1932), does he intend to show Trotsky preparing to tear his eyes out? Is this construable as historical pretext? A curious effect of this photograph's development is its (inadvertent?) constructivist composition.

Ramón Mercader's actions are traceable, by his own admission, through a series of lookings and not-lookings. The camera here evidences a murder of sorts in that it "records our likeness without returning our gaze." [95]

»

95   Walter Benjamin, "On some motifs in Baudelaire" in *Illuminations*, 188.

I waited and waited.

»

What was he reading?

»

A life thus weighted is not a life. But tendered between waiting and will. Waiting, after all, has its share of will. And will its necessity for waiting.

»

"For if the sentence is the wall", [96]

96   Walter Benjamin, "The Task of the Translator" in *Illuminations*, 79.

»

a drowned city or an atelier.

»

The angle of the door is an oblique referent. An oxygen tank fastened to a wheelchair is equivalent to approximately two hours and forty-five minutes worth of deliberations and paint scrapings. Its colour is taped shut. The stairs from the ground floor remain uncounted, notwithstanding the undescribed assailant. The bench in the hallway is painted white. The line is cut at 11:38 am. A misrecorded hour. We are survived by no one.

»

Fortified by its constructs, V. I. Arnold's theory of catastrophies is described as being comprised of discontinuities characterised by violence. Inflected against an obstructed throat, it measures up to its own indescribability.

»

The fault line is indivisible. It proceeds at an undisclosed rate toward a point that escapes mechanical fixation.

»

Room: une pièce.

»

Suffused with caffeinated milk and opiates.

Bottles and vials and droppers and straws.

»

The nominal clutch is juridical. It is not clear who, of Cain or Abel, is culpable, nor whether a name is capable of settling a death. [97]

»

August: The Ionnis Xenakis exhibition is concurrent with the windows exhibition at the architectural museum. The latter is comprised of a single wall of three poorly lit glass cases (windows). Most of the documents have been removed because of the high humidity of summer. Among the windowed "windows", there is a photograph of Mies van der Rohe overlooking his Chicago. The city is recognisable by his cigar. Among the transcripts, drawings and recordings of Xenakis, there is Nuits (1967), a composition for twelve mixed soloist voices. The "obscure political prisonners" named in the dedication are Narcisso Julian (Spain), detained since 1946, Costa Philinis (Greece) since 1947, Eli Erythriadou (Greece) since 1950, Joachim Amaro (Portugal) since

97 "Pour la première fois mon nom ne nomme pas." Marguerite Duras, *Le ravissement de Lol V. Stein*, 113.

1952, and the "millions of forgotten ones whose very names have been lost."

»

Among the lost names is the rue Baile, also, beneath an arbor, in the rain.

»

Between 1903 and 1906, Brazilian photographer Marc Ferrez was commissioned to photograph the development of Rio de Janeiro's Avenida Central, today Avenida Rio Branco. Two kilometres long by thirty-three metres large, the renovation of the street entailed the expropriation of 1,700 properties and the razing of 500 buildings, displacing some 4,000 people. To ensure the preservation of his work, Ferrez used collotypes instead of albumen prints, a technique more resistant to the region's high humidity. Despite these precautionary efforts, most of the 110 copies of the albums he had printed were destroyed by a flood.

»

Une pièce de théâtre.

»

The darkroom is barricaded. In the manner of the boulevards, it gathers into itself the space of refusal, warded off at its periphery. The photographer lies unconscious on the floor. Does she repudiate a mode of production (reproduction)? The stack of undeveloped papers in the freezer marks the desuetude of mechanical function. There are wooden clothes pegs on a line.

»

The call comes in the midst of the Joseph Cornell boxes.

»

Ein Stück.

»

The metonymic transfer evident in Cartier-

Bresson's portraits bearing place names in the place of the names of people is not a form of universality. Rather they posit the anonymity of suffering.

»

For example: Deßau, Germany, 1945.

»

If I write the photographer, do I do the photographer a wrong?

VI (b)

If it is true that "le réel ne cesse jamais de 'brûler l'image'" [98], then the burnt image forfeits the real in keeping with the execution of the real as it happens.

98   Walter Benjamin as quoted by Georges Didi-Huberman in *Devant le temps*, 235.

»

An effect of its elusiveness.

»

The photographic fixation with fixity [99] is likely an expression of disappointment. The photograph is concerned primarily with what disappears from view. In this it is a near perfect expression of desire.

99   "'Fixed' means outlined, admitted into the boundary (*peras*), brought into the outline—" Martin Heidegger, tr. Albert Hofstadter.

»

Its unrecognisability, for example.

»

The present of the photograph is no more documentable than is the present of a book as it is written. If it is a document at all, it is a document of its failure to keep time.

»

Viktor Kossakovksy's *Tishe!* may serve as an example of such a failure: the present as it is kept through the filmmaker's slumbering vigil. Sleeping then startled.

»

Near because it maintains at all times an unappreciable distance from its objective and from itself.

»

In this very way does contemporary philosophy fail at articulating the present of speaking. A reliance on antecedents (with its concern for juridical precedence) exposes the vacuity of (over-) thought.

»

Objectionable   because   its   objective [100] is

flawed. Flawed in that it seeks perfection.

»

Its claim to contemporaneity may itself be suspect.

»

"We all tramped the streets trying to find rooms in which to stay." [101]

101   Bertrand Russell, as cited by Ray Monk, 210.

»

There are no smooth surfaces worth mention-ing. Geometry's sufficiencies cast mortality against temporal perversion. Where it seeks to remove an obstacle, the obstacle becomes a means in itself.

»

A geometry of duress: A cashmere scarf dam-aged in two parts; at the nape and at the heart.

»

Bachmann: "It must be concluded that both rock formations must have suffered (suffered!) a final metamorphism, and likewise a mechanical realignment as a result of a subsequent overthrust." [102]

102   *The Book of Franza*, 49.

»

For each time that the frame falls from the shelf, the letter is shaken. The margin redresses itself. And the glass, though it does not break, comes away from the masonite back, creating a gap through which a piece of time becomes visible.

»

For having been this long suspended.

»

When you first write me in 2007 I remember you as someone.

»

It moves further and further to the rightmost edge, tilting upwards, drowning in it.

»

"…on ne devient pas seulement adulte sous les bombardements." [103]

103   Miriam Cendrars. "À voix nue," *France Culture*, 18 janvier 2011.

»

To introduce an exergue this late.

»

104   *The Book of Franza*, 48.

They are each leaned against the walls. Walls that might be "hanging walls" [104] had we not already imagined ourselves hanging from them. Leaned for the aberrant [105] sake of preservation, as though in keeping with the untimely notice of days, our motion to have them removed might somehow be disregarded.

105   *(OED)* 6. Optics. The non-convergence of rays of light, reflected or refracted, to one focus. That due to the failure of a spherical mirror or lens to cause all the rays to meet in a single point (as is effected by a parabolic mirror or lens) is called *spherical aberration*; the distance of any ray from the geometrical focus, when measured along the axis, is its *longitudinal* aberration,

»

and when measured at right angles to the axis, its *lateral* aberration. *Chromatic aberration* is an additional irregularity in the refraction of light through lenses, due to the different refrangibilities of the different coloured constituents of white light, whereby these diverge from one another, fringing the images of objects with the prismatic colours.

As for us, we were unregarded, but this was nothing in the way of things.

»

A temporal remove: That the disappearance of Robert Capa's *Mexican Suitcase* is revealed at the same time as the reappearance of the film proposes not only the recurrence of martial malady, but the timeliness (untimeliness) of looking.

»

A desk fire.

»

If it were I would tell you: "We are narrating something already dead, or in the process of dying." [106]

106   Rolf Borzik.

»

Time ill-fitted to the epistolary manner occasioned by it.

»

Each time, I must relearn you. There is something in it of an unresolved temporality. Or perhaps attributable to the faults in my memory.

»

"Since my return I have tried twice to play it, and again have wept." [107]

107   Shostakovich.

»

There is a concordance between this book, the string quartet n° 8, and a photograph that has been in my company since last year, Vienna.

»

Where it is obvious that the heart over-
estimates the horse, it is no doubt good to
doubt obviousness where it is foremost.

Morendo

The body is carried from the river to the bed. What light comes in is turned away at the bridge by the demonstrators. The event is not able to be photographed. Neither from atop the aluminium ladder at the loft nor from the doorway. I am on the floor as it is. There are two walls in each of which is a door. Neither leads out. The music forms a third wall, a membrane of sorts and it is this membrane in which the body is wrapped. The appropriate authorities are alerted as to the state of the body. At either door there is a hindrance. It takes the form of several inconsequential pictures hanging on the wall. In the underground the surfaces are covered. The noise rises from the platform by the stairwells. There is pounding against the walls. The body stirs as the photographs become legible. They are procedural illustrations of autopsies. It is clear that we are mistaken. It is the body of a person who is not dead. There is evidence, however, of decomposition. The pictures are not portends. They are worse than this. They are decisional in their placement and the construction that is built around them. To have entered by these doors is to have agreed to their morbid tautology. In this case and in every case it is to enter by them only.

This is architecture's reprove.

»

The French-English portion of the *Harrap's Standard Dictionary* is compiled much later than the English-French volume. One is not the simple inverse of the other. Several dates stand out as significant: the project of this dictionary began just before WWI, also known as the Great War, also referred to as the war of 14-18, etc. The first (English-French) part was published in 1934, while the second part appeared in 1939. In 1945 work on the Mansion dictionary was begun. I note these temporal coincidences, just as I note that in René Thom's interviews, he identifies the onset of Catastrophe Theory as having occurred in 1939. [108] Drawing out potentially falsely causal relations, but nonetheless relevant to considerations of language and time, what, then, is the concordance between war and language or war and geometry, or for that matter, geometry and language. The extension of each of these two arbitrarily selected projects well beyond the war periods suggests, perhaps erroneously (and for this may be

108   When asked, in an interview how it is that Thom came to choose maths over philosophy, he replies: "Surtout, nous étions en 1939, au début de la guerre. Et nos parents, qui avaient fait la Première Guerre nous disaient: tâche d'être artilleur: on y est moins exposé dans dans l'infanterie! Pour être artilleur, il fallait avoir fait des mathématiques."

deserving of even more pointed attention), that we have not yet emerged—nor may we ever do so—from the period directly succeeding it: post war, as it is lexically inscribed in our temporal habits.

»

Posed differently: Have I outlived the present? [109]

»

109   "Life seems to be a long unwritten letter and in this sense I have become—perhaps always was—damnably illiterate."

Paul Virilio is unflinching in his admonishment of futurity, and his accusation of *the instant*'s complicity with fascism. [110] What he calls "des phénomènes de futurisation" is masked by the contemporary preoccupation with *the instant*: "Donc l'instant que l'on nous propose aujourd'hui est un futurisme masqué, et les futurismes masqués mènent au fascisme, de nouveaux fascismes qui n'ont rien à voir avec les panzers, les marches au pas de l'oie, ou avec Mussolini ou Hitler, des fascismes liés au succès des techniques à cet accident..."

110   "Je rappelle que Marinetti a été un des inspirateurs du fascisme! N'oublions pas que le Blitzkrieg, elle est sortie du futurisme fasciste italien." (Warum Paul Virilio, 2008.)

»

It follows that if architecture stands against time, photography must refute it. In this do they bear a similar responsibility to the present. Their time is always faulted.

»

When I write that photography *must refute it*, do I mean to suggest that it is under an obligation to do so or that it is very likely that it will. Is likelihood a function of an injunction or a will? Is will the exercise of a freedom? Is freedom, then, a mode of photography?

»

If either were to stand for time (to stand still, that is) they would cease to function within their respective categories. Tautologically, they would exhaust themselves. For example, the time of architecture would no longer be articulable in an architecture of time. The time being being indisputable. These are not simple reversals. Nor are they folded over and over along the same crease. They are small demolitions that occur successively and whose simultaneity would simply produce vacancies.

»

Arguably, all time is simultaneity. The human insistence on measurability perhaps the most convincing case in point.

»

"Now" is simultaneously "now" and "not-now". This may otherwise be describable as a "catastrophe of the mind". [111]

111 Hilda Hilst.
"OS SENTIMENTOS
vastos não têm nome."

»

A theatre of the castrophal, with its figuring of untranslatability is also in this sense a theatre of the mind. A catastrophic theatre that exceeds thought. In other words it is unthinkable.

»

112 "La mort ne se pense pas."
(Simone de Beauvoir)

In this does it resemble death. [112]

»

It resembles death without being death, such

as it is. For example, the temporal rendering of Sophie Ristelhueber's *Fait* makes the photographer responsible for what she photographs, much as the body is responsible for what it carries. It is not that the photograph creates and unfurls its own logic. Rather that the distance between bodies becomes increasingly catastrophic.

»

Death as it is distinct from agony.

»

Agonia.

»

The instantané—*a snapshot*—is literally rendered by a curious English translation as a *momental photo*. The literalisation is in and of time. Does this make of the *moment de syncope* a refutation of time? A photograph, as it were? Incapable of a present?

»

Recusal: There is no room in a theatre of the catastrophal for belief of any kind.

»

Because the bomb shelter anticipates the bomb by its very verbiage, it contains in its structure the idea of the missile that will strike it, and by extension the abrasion of bodies.

»

113   "There is everything by which silence arrives."

"Il y a tout ce par quoi le silence arrive." [113]

»

Unless it is the belief that the belief which gives rise to it is untenable.

»

"The whole thing (I mean the sociality) makes me feel terribly ill-produced as a person. A person is not a play but the theatres are no less forensic in their persistent auscultations."

»

For example: The door opens onto nothing but itself. In this does the door imitate the function of a door without ever achieving it. It effectively destroys the possibility of traversal: [114]

»

114 In each of Nicolas Grospierre's photographic epitaphs—which anticipate, often unwittingly, the destruction of the sites already in ruin—the inside doors are open. Within the now defunct Lithuanian balneological hospital of Druskinnikai, *Hydroklinika*, the since demolished palace hotel in Warsaw, *Hotel Europesjski*, or the undisclosed embassy of an Eastern European country, all of the photographs harbour a consistently near indiscernible detail: all the doors leading into the buildings are shut such that these relics appear to be impenetrable. The interiors, however, each contain doors that open—onto nothing other than themselves. The Sartrian implications need not be belaboured.

115 James Elkins quoting from the guest book at the Rothko chapel in Texas.

"the perfect pain of being so near." [115]

»

This is the last of Sisyphus.

»

"A thrown stone and no broken glass. A silence manifest as violence." [116]

»

Still: Because you do not see it, I can, with extraordinary effort, look past it to you. I have only to turn my back on the alligators, exit through the dark door with the furnaces at my back,

»

"No. What I object to is the bridge falling down." [117]

»

A perfect wound, deeply bruised, and barely visible.

»

Complicating messagings against a self in a

116 There is no room.

117 Alan Turing.

world, a remanded language that disapproves
an I and in the midst of it the lamed travail of
speaking. "In the place of a nothing reaching,
even failingly, into something, a nothing at all.
Not even: *there was*."

, out of the compound and into the field.

Summary

V. I. Arnold. *Catastrophe Theory.* Springer-Verlag. Berlin, 1984.

Ingeborg Bachmann. *The Book of Franza & Requiem for Fanny Goldmann*, tr. Peter Filkins. Northwestern University Press. Evanston (IL), 1999; *The Thirtieth Year*, tr. Michael Bullock. Holmes & Meier. New York, 1995.

Daniel Barenboim & Eward W. Said. *Parallels and Paradoxes: Explorations in Music and Society.* Vintage. New York, 2004.

Jean Baudrillard. *Amérique*. Grasset. Paris, 1986.

Walter Benjamin. *Selected Writings, Volume 1, 1913-1926*, eds. Marcus Bullock and Michael W. Jennings. Belknap of Harvard. Cambridge (MA) and London, 1996.

Maurice Blanchot. *L'Écriture du désastre*. Gallimard. Paris, 1980; *L'arrêt de mort*. Gallimard. Paris, 1948.

Martin Buber. *Between Man and Man*, tr. Ronald Gregor-Smith. Routledge. London and New York, 2002 (1947).

Café Müller. *L'Arche*. Paris, 2010.

Cecil Scott Burgess. *Architecture, Town Planning and Community*, ed. Donald G. Wetherell. University of Alberta. Edmonton, 2005.

Robert Capa. *Robert Capa.* Pantheon Photo Library. New York, 1989; *The Mexican Suitcase*, ed. Cynthia Young. International Center for Photography + Steidl. New York + Göttingen, 2010.

Cathy Caruth. *Unclaimed Experience.* The Johns Hopkins University Press. Baltimore, 1996.

Paul Celan. *Poems of Paul Celan*, tr. Michael Hamburger. Persea. New York, 1995.

CNAC. *Vieira da Silva : Peintures, 1935 à 1969.* Musée National d'Art Moderne. Paris, 1969.

Mahmoud Darwish. *Memory for Forgetfulness: August, Beirut, 1982*, tr. Ibrahim Muhawi. University of California Press. Berkeley (CA), 1995.

Jacques Derrida. *Chaque fois unique la fin du monde.* Galilée. Paris, 2003; *Donner la mort.* Galilée. Paris, 1999; *Was ist Dichtung?* Brinkmann & Bose. Berlin, 1990.

Marguerite Duras. *Le Ravissement de Lol V. Stein.* Gallimard. Paris, 1964.

James Elkins. *"Camera Dolorosa"*. *History of Photography*, Vol. 31, N° 1. Spring 2007; *Pictures and Tears*. Routledge. New York and London, 2001.

Funk & Wagnalls New Standard Encyclopedia. New York + London, 1931.

Hervé Guibert. *Le mausolée des amants, Journal 1976–1991*. Gallimard. Paris, 2001.

Martin Heidegger. "Building, Dwelling, Thinking" and "The Origin of the Work of Art", tr. Albert Hofstadter. *Basic Writings*. Harper San Francisco. New York, 2008 (1977).

Hilda Hilst. *A obscena Senhora D.* Editora Globo. São Paolo, 2001 (1982); *Rútilo Nada*. Pontes. Campinas, 1993.

Guy Hocquenghem. *Le désir homosexuel*. Fayard. Paris, 1972.

Hans Höller, Helga Pöcheim, Karl Solibakke (Hg.). *Ingeborg Bachmann: Schreiben gegen den Krieg / Writing against War*. Erhard Löcker. Wien, 2008.

Eugéne Ionesco. *Notes et contre-notes*. Gallimard. Paris, 1966.

James Joyce. *Ulysses*. Vintage. New York, 1914 / 1961.

Alexander Kluge. *Case Histories.* tr. Leila Vennewitz. Homes & Meier. London + New York, 1991 [1988].

Arthur Koestler / Albert Camus. *Réflexions sur la peine capitale.* Gallimard. Paris, 1957 / 2002.

Spiro Kostof. "His Majesty the Pick: The Aesthetics of Demolition", in *Streets: Critical Perspectives on Public Space,* eds. Zeynep Çelik, Diane Favro, Richard Ingersoll. University of California Press. Berkeley, 1994.

Karl Gernot Kuehn. *Caught: The Art of Photography in the German Democratic Republic.* University of California Press. Berkeley, 1997.

Sophie Lacroix. *Ruine.* Éditions de la Villette. Paris, 2008.

Christine Lavant. *Un art comme le mien n'est que vie mutilée,* tr. François Mathieu. Éditions Lignes. Fecamp, 2009. *Memoirs from a Madhouse,* tr. Renate Latimer. Ariadne Press. Riverside (CA), 2004.

Michel Lussault. *L'homme spatial.* Éditions du Seuil. Paris, 2007.

135

Jean-François Lyotard. *Soundproof Room: Malraux's Anti-Aesthetics*. Stanford University Press. Stanford (CA), 2001.

Paul de Man. "Conclusions" on Walter Benjamin's "The Task of the Translator" Messenger Lecture, Cornell University, March 4, 1983. *Yale French Studies*, Nº 97, *50 Years of Yale French Studies: A Commemorative Anthology*. Part 2, 1980–1998 (2000).

Patrick Maynard. *The Engine of Visualization: Thinking through Photography*. Cornell University Press. Ithaca (NY), 1997.

Ray Monk. *Ludwig Wittgenstein: The Duty of Genius*. Penguin. New York, 1990.

Stephen Motika. *Arrival and At Mono*. Sona Books. Brooklyn (NY), 2007.

Museum Ludwig Cologne. *20th Century Photography*. Taschen. Köln, 2001.

Friedrich Nietzsche. *Untimely Meditations*, tr. R. J. Hollingdale. Cambridge University Press. New York, 1983.

Yuriy Norshteyn. *Hedgehog in the Fog*, 1975.

Michael O'Leary. *Along the Chess Pavilion.* LVNG Supplemental Series, Nº 9. Chicago, undated.

Oxford English Dictionary Online. Second Edition 1989, Oxford University Press, 2009.

Michael Palmer. *Sun.* North Point. San Francisco (CA), 1988.

Personal Correspondence. John Beer, Amina Cain, Joel Felix, Suzanne Jacob, RY King, Benny Nemerofsky Ramsay, Jennifer Scappettone, Brian Teare, Yaël Weiss.

Marie-Françoise Plissart. *Droit de regards suivi d'une lecture par Jacques Derrida.* Minuit. Paris, 1985.

Dmitri Shostakovich. *Quartet n° 8 for two violins, viola, and violoncello, Op. 110.* DSCH Publishers. Moscow, 2006.

N. *We Press Ourselves Plainly.* Nightboat Callicoon, 2010; *Carnet de désaccords.* Le Quartanier. Montréal, 2009; "Some notes on death and the burning of buildings", *inédit*, 2009; *Absence Where As (Claude Cahun and the Unopened Book).* Nightboat. New York, 2009; "The tautological fury of a disconsolate mind", in *Evening Will Come*, February 2011.

René Thom. *Prédire n'est pas expliquer*. Flammarion. Paris, 1993.

Ilsa Trudel. *Walter Benjamin : l'ange assassiné*. Mengès. Paris, 2006.

Paul Virilio. *Bunker Archéologie*. Galilée. Paris, 2008; *Bunker Archeology*, tr. George Collins. Princeton Architectural Press. New York, 1994.

Dmitri Volkogonov. *Trotsky: The Eternal Revolutionary*. Free Press. New York, 1996.

Ludwig Wittgenstein. *Philosophical Remarks*, ed. Rush Rhees, tr. Raymond Hargreaves and Roger White. University of Chicago Press. Chicago, 1975.

Translations

Translations are attributable to N. unless otherwise indicated.

René Thom

> It may be possible to demonstrate the incontrovertible character of certain catastrophes, like illness or death. Knowledge will no longer necessarily be a promise of success, or of survival; it may just as easily be the certainty of our failure, of our end.

Equation of dynamic crack growth
Transcription by Michael O'Leary

Michel Lussault

> ...the verb to exist retrieves its first significance, if we return to the etymology of *ex-istere*. *Sistere*, which is derived from the Indo-European root *sta*, which means to stand upright, unmoving (whence the Latin stare), signifies to place and/or to place onself. To exist is thus to place and/or to place oneself "*ex*"—outside of: both to place and to displace onself, in short to find one's (rightful) places.
> »
> But a seism in itself is not a social phenomenon.

Jacques Derrida

You hear the catastrophe coming.

»

Your heart beats you.

René Thom

...the modes by which one space can be sent into another.

Guy Hocquenghem

[Homosexual desire] is the slope towards trans-sexuality through the disappearance of objects and subjects, the slide towards the discovery that in matters of sex everything communicates.

Hervé Guibert

Since photography can only be an event of light, without a subject (and it is then that it is at its most photographic), I would like one day to launch myself into a narrative that would be nothing but an event of writing, without a story, and without boredom, a true adventure.

Jean-François Lyotard

...sexuality, independent of any object. (Tr. Robert Harvey)

»

...subject or rejection (Idem)

Sophie Lacroix
> The ruin leads us to an experience which is that of the relinquished subject, and paradoxically this experience has no object.

Hervé Guibert
> ...I need catastrophes, *coups de théâtre*.

Jean-François Lyotard
> ...the annihilation annihilated, the end deprived of itself." (*Idem*)
>
> »
>
> ...the lucid dread of redundancy. (*Idem*)

Maurice Blanchot
> Disaster is separate; that which is most separate. (Tr. Ann Smock. I note with interest, Smock's insertion of the semi-colon, making more distinct the separation between clauses.)

N.
> Je n'en peux plus d'être le meurtrier.
>
> »
>
> A syncope in the blood.

René Thom
> What is usually referred to as a form is always, in the final analysis, a qualitative

142

discontinuity on some continuous
ground.

»

The distance between a personal conviction
and its demonstration is enormous:

Albert Camus

My mother relates merely that he came
rushing home, his face distorted, refused
to talk, lay down for a moment on the bed,
and suddenly began to vomit. … Instead of
thinking of slaughtered children, he could
think of nothing but that quivering body
that had just been dropped onto a board
to have its head cut off. (Tr. Justin O'Brien)

André Malraux

Nothing remains of this event. (Tr.
Terence Kilmartin)

»

History obliterates even men's forgetfulness. [forgetting] *(Idem)*

»

On the birth day of my fortieth year, as I
was clandestinely crossing the demarca-
tion line with the black cat, I would have
wanted to have been born yesterday.

René Thom

There is no escaping the continuum.

Hervé Guibert
> One day, all the photos will have dis-
> solved, the photographic paper will no
> longer impress, react, will be a dead thing.

Hilda Hilst
> I don't understand the eye, and I'm trying
> to get closer.

André Malraux
> A feeling without an object, like anguish,
> and which invents its object.

Suzanne Jacob
> I wish I could wail out of all nine windows
> and three doors of this house without
> heirs. (Tr. Luise von Flotow)

Jean Baudrillard
> There, space is thought itself.

André Bazin
> ...to save (the) being by appearances.

Georges Didi-Huberman
> It could be thought of as a moment, as
> a rhythmic beat of method, were it its
> moment of syncope.

Maurice Blanchot
> But a thought is not altogether a person,

Malraux

During the Resistance, for two years I had in my possession some cyanide. When London distributed it to us, I asked myself whether the scene from my book would not become premonitory.

Michel Lussault and Jacques Lévy

The distinction between 'natural' and anthropic risks, for example, becomes difficult to establish due to the growing transformation of bio-physical environments, except in certain simple situations such as seisms or volcanic erruptions.

Barbey d'Aurevilly

The dandy is of an undecided intellectual sex.

Jacques Derrida

This trembling seizes one at the moment of becoming a person, (Tr. David Wills)

Marguerite Duras

But what is suffering without a subject?

Eugène Ionesco

The tragic character does not change, he breaks; he is him, he is real.

Duras
> For the first time my name does not name.

Walter Benjamin
> The real ceases to 'burn the image'.

Miriam Cendrars
> ...one does not only become an adult under the bombings.

Score

Shostakovich's string quartet n° 8, Op. 110, was "composed in the summer of 1960 while he was visiting

Памяти жертв фашизма и войны

КВАРТЕТ № 8

Соч. 110 (1960)

Dresden. Shostakovich's distress at the extent of the city's devastation was so profound that he wrote this quartet in only a few days and dedicated it to the 'victims of fascism and war'" (Antje Schneider, tr. Susan Kunst-Elliott). Rudolf Barshai's transcription for string orchestra is known as Chamber Symphony, Op. 110 a.

René Thom
> More than anything, it was 1939, the beginning of the war. And our parents,

who had fought in the First War were saying to us: make sure you're an artilleryman: you'll be less exposed than in the infantry! To be an artilleryman, you needed to have studied mathematics.

Paul Virilio

Remember that Marinetti was one inspiration for Fascism! Let's not forget that the Blitzkrieg emerged from fascist Italian Futurism. (Tr. undisclosed).

»

...phenomena of futurisation... *(Idem)*

»

Therefore, the moment as proposed today is a masked futurism and these masked futurisms lead to Fascism, new fascisms which have nothing to do with panzers, goose stepping, Mussolini or Hitler, but are fascisms linked to technical achievements, to this accident... *(Idem)*

Hilda Hilst

VAST EMOTIONS have no name.

Simone de Beauvoir

Death is unthinkable.

$$\frac{\partial^2 L_c}{\partial \dot{\ell}^2} \ddot{\ell} = \frac{\partial L_c}{\partial \ell} - \frac{\partial^2 L_c}{\partial \ell \partial \dot{\ell}} \dot{\ell}$$

Images, in order of appearance

Equation of Dynamic Crack Growth, Michael O'Leary (frontispiece)

Untitled, RY King, 2008.

Une mer attendue / An ocean that doesn't arrive, N. after RY, 2010.

Idem (detail).

Quartet n° 8 for two violins, viola and violoncello, Opus 110 (score; detail), Dmitri Shostakovich, 1960.

River Tay Bridge, James Valentine, 1880.

Nathanaël is the author of a score of books written in English or French, including *We Press Ourselves Plainly*, *Carnet de somme*, *Paper City*, and *L'injure*. *Je Nathanaël* exists in self-translation, as does the essay of correspondence, *Absence Where As (Claude Cahun and the Unopened Book)*, first published in French as *L'absence au lieu*. There is a book of talks, *At Alberta*. Some texts exist in Basque, Slovene, and Spanish (Mexico), with book-length translations in Bulgarian and Portuguese (Brazil). In addition to her self-translations, Nathanaël has translated Édouard Glissant, Catherine Mavrikakis, and Hilda Hilst, the latter in collaboration with Rachel Gontijo Araújo. She lives in Chicago.

© 2012 by Nathanaël
Printed in the United States

ISBN 978–1–937658–05–2

Design and Typesetting
Mark Addison Smith
Text set in DIN

Cover art
Equation of Dynamic Crack Growth (detail)
Michael O'Leary

Cataloging-in-publication data is available
from the Library of Congress

Distributed by the University Press of New England
One Court Street
Lebanon, NH 03766
www.upne.com

Nightboat Books
Callicoon, New York
www.nightboat.org

Nightboat Books, a nonprofit organization, seeks to develop audiences for writers whose work resists convention and transcends boundaries. We publish books rich with poignancy, intelligence, and risk. Please visit our website, www.nightboat.org, to learn about our titles and how you can support our future publications.

The following individuals have supported the publication of this book. We thank them for their generosity and commitment to the mission of Nightboat Books:

Kazim Ali

Elizabeth Motika

Benjamin Taylor

In addition, this book has been made possible, in part, by a grant from the New York State Council on the Arts Literature Program.

State of the Arts

NYSCA